FRANCIS FRITH'S

SHROPSHIRE
LIVING MEMORIES

DOROTHY NICOLLE was born in Uganda and later lived in Hong Kong. She was educated in Belfast and at Leicester University where she attained a degree in British Archaeology and History. She has also lived in the Middle East and in France. This gypsy life has encouraged a love of Britain and its history so that, these days, she knows that she has the perfect job - she is a Blue Badge Guide. She also lectures on various aspects of local and general history. Dorothy is married and now lives in Shropshire where she and her husband enjoy walking in the hills with their dogs.

FRANCIS FRITH'S
PHOTOGRAPHIC MEMORIES

FRANCIS FRITH'S

SHROPSHIRE
LIVING MEMORIES

DOROTHY NICOLLE

THE FRANCIS FRITH COLLECTION

FRITH BOOK Co

First published in the United Kingdom in 2003 by
Frith Book Company Ltd

Hardback Edition 2003
ISBN 1-85937-643-6

British Library Cataloguing in Publication Data

Francis Frith's -
Shropshire Living Memories
Dorothy Nicolle

Frith Book Company Ltd
Frith's Barn, Teffont,
Salisbury, Wiltshire SP3 5QP
Tel: +44 (0) 1722 716 376
Email: info@francisfrith.co.uk
www.francisfrith.co.uk

Printed and bound in Great Britain

Front Cover: **WHITCHURCH**, *High Street c1950* W84015

Frontispiece: **CLUN**, *The Old Bridge c1960* C507053

*The hand-colouring is for illustrative purposes only, and is not
intended to be historically accurate.*

CONTENTS

FRANCIS FRITH
VICTORIAN PIONEER

FRANCIS FRITH, founder of the world-famous photographic archive, was a complex and multi-talented man. A devout Quaker and a highly successful Victorian businessman, he was philosophic by nature and pioneering in outlook.

By 1855 he had already established a wholesale grocery business in Liverpool, and sold it for the astonishing sum of £200,000, which is the equivalent today of over £15,000,000. Now a very rich man, he was able to indulge his passion for travel. As a child he had pored over travel books written by early explorers, and his fancy and imagination had been stirred by family holidays to the sublime mountain regions of Wales and Scotland. 'What lands of spirit-stirring and enriching scenes and places!' he had written. He was to return to these scenes of grandeur in later years to 'recapture the thousands of vivid and tender memories', but with a different purpose. Now in his thirties, and captivated by the new science of photography, Frith set out on a series of pioneering journeys up the Nile and to the

Near East that occupied him from 1856 until 1860.

INTRIGUE AND EXPLORATION

These far-flung journeys were packed with intrigue and adventure. In his life story, written when he was sixty-three, Frith tells of being held captive by bandits, and of fighting 'an awful midnight battle to the very point of surrender with a deadly pack of hungry, wild dogs'. Wearing flowing Arab costume, Frith arrived at Akaba by camel seventy years before Lawrence of Arabia, where he encountered 'desert princes and rival sheikhs, blazing with jewel-hilted swords'.

He was the first photographer to venture beyond the sixth cataract of the Nile. Africa was still the mysterious 'Dark Continent', and Stanley and Livingstone's historic meeting was a decade into the future. The conditions for picture taking confound belief. He laboured for hours in his wicker dark-room in the sweltering heat of the desert, while the volatile chemicals fizzed dangerously in their trays. Back in London he exhibited his photographs and was 'rapturously cheered' by members of the Royal Society. His reputation as a photographer was made overnight.

VENTURE OF A LIFE-TIME

Characteristically, Frith quickly spotted the opportunity to create a new business as a specialist publisher of photographs. He lived in an era of immense and sometimes violent change.

For the poor in the early part of Victoria's reign work was exhausting and the hours long, and people had precious little free time to enjoy themselves. Most had no transport other than a cart or gig at their disposal, and rarely travelled far beyond the boundaries of their own town or village. However, by the 1870s the railways had threaded their way across the country, and Bank Holidays and half-day Saturdays had been made obligatory by Act of Parliament. All of a sudden the working man and his family were able to enjoy days out and see a little more of the world.

With typical business acumen, Francis Frith foresaw that these new tourists would enjoy having souvenirs to commemorate their days out. In 1860 he married Mary Ann Rosling and set out on a new career: his aim was to photograph every city, town and village in Britain. For the next thirty years he travelled the country by train and by pony and trap, producing fine photographs of seaside resorts and beauty spots that were keenly bought by millions of Victorians. These prints were painstakingly pasted into family albums and pored over during the dark nights of winter, rekindling precious memories of summer excursions.

THE RISE OF FRITH & CO

Frith's studio was soon supplying retail shops all over the country. To meet the demand he gathered about him a small team of photographers, and published the work of independent artist-photographers of the calibre of Roger Fenton and Francis Bedford. In order to gain some understanding of the scale of Frith's business one only has to look at the catalogue issued by Frith & Co in 1886: it runs to some 670 pages, listing not only many thousands of views of the British Isles but also many photographs of most European countries, and China, Japan, the USA and Canada - note the sample page shown on page 9 from the hand-written Frith & Co ledgers recording the pictures. By 1890 Frith had created the greatest specialist photographic publishing company in the world, with over 2,000 sales outlets - more than the combined number that Boots and WH Smith have today! The picture on the next page shows the Frith & Co display board at Ingleton in the Yorkshire Dales (left of window). Beautifully constructed with a mahogany frame and gilt inserts, it could display up to a dozen local scenes.

POSTCARD BONANZA

The ever-popular holiday postcard we know today took many years to develop. In 1870 the Post Office issued the first plain cards, with a pre-printed stamp on one face. In 1894 they allowed other publishers' cards to be sent through the mail with an attached adhesive halfpenny stamp. Demand grew rapidly, and in 1895 a new size of postcard was permitted called the court card, but there was little room for illustration. In 1899, a year after Frith's death, a new card measuring 5.5 x 3.5 inches became the standard format, but it was not until 1902 that the divided back came into being, so that the address and message could be on one face and a full-size illustration on the other. Frith & Co were in the vanguard of postcard development: Frith's sons Eustace and Cyril continued their father's monumental task, expanding the number of views offered to the public and recording more and more places in Britain, as the coasts and countryside were opened up to mass travel.

Francis Frith had died in 1898 at his villa in Cannes, his great project still growing. The archive he created continued in business for another seventy years. By 1970 it contained over a third of a million pictures showing 7,000 British towns and villages.

FRANCIS FRITH'S LEGACY

Frith's legacy to us today is of immense significance and value, for the magnificent archive of evocative photographs he created provides a unique record of change in the cities, towns and villages throughout Britain over a century and more. Frith and his fellow studio photographers revisited locations many times down the years to update their views, compiling for us an enthralling and colourful pageant of British life and character.

We are fortunate that Frith was dedicated to recording the minutiae of everyday life. For it is this sheer wealth of visual data, the painstaking chronicle of changes in dress, transport, street layouts, buildings, housing, engineering and landscape that captivates us so much today. His remarkable images offer us a powerful link with the past and with the lives of our ancestors.

THE VALUE OF THE ARCHIVE TODAY

Computers have now made it possible for Frith's many thousands of images to be accessed almost instantly. Frith's images are increasingly used as visual resources, by social historians, by researchers into genealogy and ancestry, by architects and town planners, and by teachers involved in local history projects.

In addition, the archive offers every one of us an opportunity to examine the places where we and our families have lived and worked down the years. Highly successful in Frith's own era, the archive is now, a century and more on, entering a new phase of popularity. Historians consider the Francis Frith Collection to be of prime national importance. It is the only archive of its kind remaining in private ownership. Francis Frith's archive is now housed in an historic timber barn in the beautiful village of Teffont in Wiltshire. Its founder would not recognize the archive office as it is today. In place of the many thousands of dusty boxes containing glass plate negatives and an all-pervading odour of photographic chemicals, there are now ranks of computer screens. He would be amazed to watch his images travelling round the world at unimaginable speeds through internet lines.

The archive's future is both bright and exciting. Francis Frith, with his unshakeable belief in making photographs available to the greatest number of people, would undoubtedly approve of what is being done today with his lifetime's work. His photographs depicting our shared past are now bringing pleasure and enlightenment to millions around the world a century and more after his death.

SHROPSHIRE
AN INTRODUCTION

The county of Shropshire has been in existence for well over 1,000 years. Throughout that time, those people living in the county have been witness to many changes. Soon after the Battle of Hastings in 1066 the Norman invaders arrived. Their presence was quickly felt in the local countryside with the establishment of first their wooden and then their stone castles, from where they controlled the local populace. Towns and churches that had already been established in Saxon times were soon expanding, while new towns, such as those at Ludlow and Newport, were established.

The area thrived. At first it was the agricultural produce that was important, but before long the wool trade developed; it far exceeded all other produce in terms of the wealth that it brought, not just to Shropshire, but also to all of England. On occasion times could be hard. As in so much of England, the Black Death badly

STOKESAY, *The Castle c1955* S202001

affected the county in the 14th century - indeed, some villages disappeared altogether. Furthermore, as a border county this region suffered regularly in medieval times from Welsh incursions. Fighting returned to Shropshire in the 17th century during the period of the Civil War.

It was the following century that was to see the greatest changes, however, when the Industrial Revolution began in Shropshire. Its effect would be felt all over the world. But before long, Shropshire's place as a world leader in the development of new technology was to be surpassed, and the county was to return once more to depend on its old sources of wealth - agricultural produce.

In the years that followed the Second World War, the period in which the photographs in this book were all taken, no-one could have ever anticipated all the changes that were soon to come. Indeed, the forty years or so since these photographs were taken have been a time of enormous change for everyone. Not only can ordinary individuals travel around the world more easily and cheaply than ever before, but also men have even gone to the moon and back. Computers and mobile phones, fridge-freezers and microwave ovens have totally changed the way in which we all live. Most of these changes could never have been envisaged by those people pictured in the photographs in this book during the 1950s and 1960s.

Shropshire has seen its own changes in this period too. If you ask the local people, these changes are not regarded as having been necessarily all for the good. For one thing, the population has grown enormously as a result of the development of an entirely new town, Telford - something that many Salopians have still not come totally to terms with.

In the years immediately after the Second World War, the area that we now know as Telford consisted of a number of small towns and villages separated by farmland. Within these towns there were a variety of industries. Although it was around this time that many of the last local mines began to close down, other industries had evolved to provide employment - industries such as steel pressing, and the production of cookers and boilers, pipes and bricks, and tools and tiles. The countryside between the towns supported thriving farms. The Telford area was hardly the 'waste land' implied by the government of the day when they selected it as suitable for the building of a new town.

The idea for a new town here was first suggested in 1955 by a journalist, A W Bowdler, in an article in the Birmingham Gazette. The population in Birmingham and the Black Country region was growing rapidly, and land was desperately required for housing. Bowdler suggested in his article that the area around Dawley would be suitable, and the government ordered feasibility studies to be carried out.

The people of Dawley (or their councillors at least) saw this as an excellent opportunity for their town. The people of Birmingham saw it (according to some) as an excellent means of ridding themselves of many of their worst problems! But not everyone liked the idea. A Dawley Development Corporation was set up to implement the government's plans. It held many 'consultation' meetings, where the planners simply announced what they were planning to do and local people were allowed to make their comments - which were then patently ignored. It is undoubtedly true that the new town was developed largely by people with next to no local knowledge, or interest, in the area.

Meantime, with so much investment in Dawley, other local authorities in the towns around (such as Wellington and Oakengates particularly) were told to delay any plans that they might have for expansion or improvements of their own. People in these towns were infuriated, but since the government controlled the finances, they had little choice but to obey. Eventually it was decided by the government that the new town would not just consist of Dawley and the country immediately around it, but would take over a much larger area of around 30 square miles altogether.

Then, there was the question of what to call this new town. The people of Dawley, who were already calling it Dawley New Town, naturally felt that this name should continue. Those who lived in Wellington (or Madeley, or Oakengates, or Malinslee, or any one of the 60 or so other towns and villages in the area) totally disagreed. Everyone argued over the new name. After a great deal of discussion, agreement was finally reached - the new town would be called Wrekin, after the great hill that overlooks it. Indeed, it would be an excellent continuation of an old tradition, since it was this hill that nearly 2,000 years ago had given its name to the large Roman settlement that had previously dominated the region - Viroconium.

Meantime, the government had been deciding on a name of their own, and suddenly announced that the new town in Shropshire would be named Telford, after Thomas Telford. But although he was Shropshire's County Surveyor for many years, and had left much of his work in evidence throughout the county, he was not even from Shropshire - he had, in fact,

come from Scotland. George Evans, in his book 'Telford's Living Landscape', describes the choice of name as a 'public relations disaster', which it most certainly was. Moreover, as Evans also says, it only served to emphasise to local people how little say they were being allowed concerning the plans for this new town that was being foisted upon them.

However, that all happened over 30 years ago. People have settled there who have never known it by any other name. A new generation has grown up that has always lived in Telford. The town is slowly beginning to develop a personality of its own. Telford is a town that has been planned for a population of car owners, with wide roads linking all the old settlements to the various new shopping and industrial centres. There are now a number of industrial estates. Following enormous investment, new industries (many of them hi-tech) have come to the area; thus although it was originally planned as a dormitory town serving the Birmingham conurbation, Telford has itself now become a focus for commuters.

One site that has particularly benefited from this investment has been the area around Ironbridge. This is an area of immense historic interest: it was here in 1709 that Abraham Darby I began to smelt iron using coke as opposed to charcoal, and so ushered in the Industrial Revolution. The modern world may have begun here, but it was not long before the focus for industry in Britain moved east to the Black Country and then spread out from there. By the end of the 1800s, Ironbridge had long since become something of an industrial backwater, and its decline was well under way.

By the 1960s this whole area was totally run

down, and nobody appeared to be very interested in it. The bridge itself fell into disrepair; in 1931 it was closed to vehicular traffic, although people could continue to walk across it if they paid their penny. Believe it or not, the decision was even made to pull the bridge down. Fortunately this period was also to see the development of an interest in industrial archaeology, and efforts were made to save not only the bridge but other sites of interest locally.

In 1967 the Ironbridge Gorge Museum Trust was established, and large sums of money were set aside for a project that was to give the town a degree of historical respectability. In the early 1970s the bridge was itself totally restored - this included a great deal of work under the river to secure its foundations. Today, the Ironbridge Gorge is a World Heritage Site attracting numerous visitors from all around the globe. The Trust continues to run a number of museums, and in 2002 a new museum called Enginuity, an interactive technology museum, was opened - it explains many of the processes behind scientific principles and technology.

This recent growth of the area around Telford has meant that today it competes with the traditional county capital, Shrewsbury, in all respects. For example, in recent years both towns have applied for (and failed to acquire) city status. Telford has certainly long since taken over as the largest centre of population as well as of industry in the county. Things recently came to a head in 1998 when there was a decision to divide Shropshire into two areas, the county of Shropshire and the Borough of Telford and Wrekin, thus bringing to an end over 1,000 years of political unity.

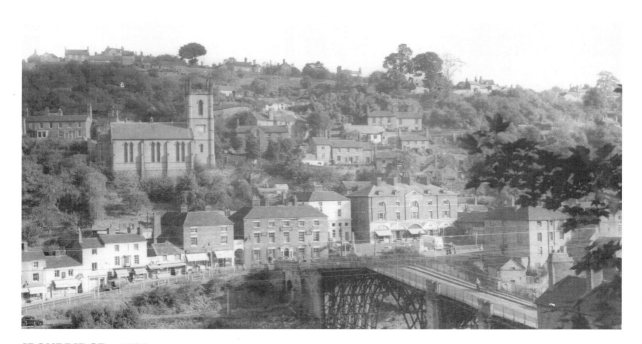

IRONBRIDGE, *c1960* I20055

SHREWSBURY AND THE FARMING COMMUNITIES OF THE NORTH

SHREWSBURY, *The Castle c1960* S125088

The town of Shrewsbury is almost completely encircled by the River Severn. The castle was built by the newly-arrived Norman invaders to control the only landward entrance into the town, from the north. Today it overlooks the railway station, whose car park we can see here.

SHREWSBURY
The Square c1960
S125109e

Now totally pedestrianised with trees planted to give some shade, the Square is dominated by the 16th-century market hall (left) and the statue of Robert Clive, Clive of India. He was born near Market Drayton, and on his return from India he became both mayor of the town and its MP.

SHREWSBURY, *The Lion Hotel c1955* S125057

An old coaching inn, the Lion Hotel (on the left of the road) was particularly famous in the 18th and 19th centuries for the regularity of its stagecoach service linking Shrewsbury with London. Charles Dickens once stayed here and wrote: 'We have the strangest little room. The windows bulge out over the street as if they were the stern windows of a ship.'

▼ **LLYNCLYS,** *A View on Llynclys Hill c1960* L545008

Llynclys Hill, to the south of Oswestry, is now a nature reserve covering an area of 40 hectares. Offa's Dyke runs along the hill at the top of a steep cliff on its western side, giving extensive views into the Welsh borderlands for those walkers who follow the Offa's Dyke Trail.

► **LLYNCLYS**
The Post Office c1960
L545014

The post office we see here on the right is now a private house; the door between the windows has been blocked up, leaving an entrance only from the side. There is still a pub in the village, however. The White Lion, the white building we can see on the left of the road, stands overlooking the road junction.

◄ OSWESTRY
Llwyd Mansion
c1960 O63100

Sitting as it does on the English-Welsh border, Oswestry was often attacked. The town therefore has few really old buildings - Llwyd Mansion is one of these, dating from 1604. Today the building is called the Heritage Gallery, and houses a gift shop. The road on the left, Bailey Street, leads to the bailey of the old castle, and is now a pedestrianised shopping area.

► OSWESTRY
Cross Street c1965
O63098

When considerably enlarged, this photograph shows a pub sign on the right depicting two crossed keys - the Keys. The pub still has the same name today, but the spelling has changed, so that it is now called the Quays - a somewhat inappropriate name for a pub in a town that is totally land-locked.

▶ **OSWESTRY**
Leg Street c1960
O63097

Soon after this photograph was taken, two employees from the branch of Woolworth's in Oswestry started 'moonlighting' by selling frozen food from the shop next door to Queens Stores, just beyond the RAC sign. They lost their jobs with Woolworth's, but went on to establish another well-known shop name - Iceland. Notice also the fake painted window on the top floor of the building opposite.

◀ **OSWESTRY**
The Wynnstay Hotel c1955 O63063

The hotel here dates from 1727, and was originally called the Bowling Green; today's hotel still has a bowling green at the back. It became a major coaching inn on the London-Holyhead road in the early 1800s. One eminent visitor was Princess Victoria, who stayed here in 1832. Such a large crowd came to see her that one woman was killed in the crush.

▲ **OSWESTRY,** *The Cattle Market c1960* O63107

As I write this, the 2001 outbreak of foot and mouth disease is a very recent and raw memory for farmers in Shropshire, and its repercussions are still to be fully understood. This view shows the old cattle market, close to the centre of town, with the spire of Holy Trinity Church in the background.

◀ **OSWESTRY**
The Robert Jones and Agnes Hunt Orthopaedic Hospital, Kenyon and Gladstone Wards c1960 O63071

Everyone is out in the sunshine. Notice how the ward on the right has louvred doors, while the ward on the left has tarpaulin curtains but no doors. Each ward was built like this, with one wall with louvred doors and one wall with curtains. Dame Agnes Hunt, one of the founders of the hospital, was a firm believer in the good effects of fresh air, so much so that her first hospital here (founded in 1921) had wards with entire walls missing. In winter this meant that nurses sometimes had to tend their patients while walking on duckboards to keep their feet out of the slushy snow. Today this has become one of the world's leading orthopaedic hospitals.

▼ **BRONYGARTH,** *The Post Office c1955* B863012

This is now a private house called Rose Cottage; the building has been painted white, and is almost completely unrecognisable, with just its roofline remaining the same. The trees in the background have grown over what was once a quarry; evidence for it survives in nearby lime kilns, which can be seen from the road.

► **WESTON RHYN**
Chirk Castle from Bronygarth c1950
W567003

Bronygarth sits across the England-Wales border, which at this point follows the line of the River Ceirog in the valley. At the other side, on a superb site, sits Chirk Castle, once a stronghold of the Mortimer family and now run by the National Trust. It is surprising to see that the open area of land immediately around and below the castle is now completely covered by very well established woodland.

◀ **WESTON RHYN**
The Lodge Inn
c1950 W567010

Weston Rhyn developed as a small village where five roads met, and the Lodge Inn was therefore positioned overlooking the road junction, where it could benefit from the passing trade. In the grounds of a house nearby is Shropshire's own Stonehenge - actually it is a Victorian folly built for Thomas Barnes, who retired here having made his fortune in railways and cotton mills.

▶ **WESTON RHYN**
The County School
c1950 W567009

Now known as the Weston Rhyn Primary School, the school was built in 1924. Today there are around 160 pupils here drawn from quite a large area. The village has recently grown enormously following the building of a dual carriageway linking the area with Wrexham and Chester, and many people from here now commute to those towns.

GOBOWEN
The Cross c1955
G234008

This photograph looks towards the level crossing, where at the moment we can just see a steam train drawing away from the station. The railway station, a lovely old Italianate-style building dating from 1848, was on the verge of being closed in the mid 1990s; it was only saved by children from the school, who ran it for a time.

▶ **GOBOWEN**
The Cross c1960
G234018

The Co-operative is now the Silo Central, an internet café. There is another café just outside the village, at Derwen College. This is a college for school leavers with learning difficulties, and catering is one of the subjects taught here. The café, run by the students, recently won an award as the best in the Midlands in a competition by BBC Midlands Today.

◀ **WHITTINGTON**
The Castle c1955
W585004

It is a remarkable fact that there is known to have been a castle on this site in Saxon times. The gatehouse shown here, however, dates only from the early 1200s. In the 1700s the site of the ruined castle was laid out as a 'fancy garden', and there are now hopes that this might be restored.

▲ **WHITTINGTON,** *The Village c1955* W585005

The road sign indicates the directions to Shrewsbury and Oswestry. Since this photograph was taken, the route of the road at this point has been altered, so that it now goes through the trees. This has opened up the view considerably, so that little, apart from The White Lion pub on the right, is now easily recognisable.

◀ **ELLESMERE**
Scotland Street c1955
E180061

Despite its name, this is the main road into Ellesmere from the west, in other words from Wales. The view is very much the same today, although the grand, colonnaded entrance to The Black Lion Hotel (centre left) has been demolished. The shop beside the two girls on the left is now a restaurant and part of The Black Lion.

ELLESMERE
High Street c1955 E180086

Traffic through Ellemere's narrow streets can be difficult, and it is interesting to be reminded that this was already a problem in the 1950s - the road is one-way. At the bottom of this street is the Ellesmere Hotel. Here, in 1792, shares went on sale for the building of the Ellesmere Canal, and £1 million was raised in one day - an enormous sum for the times.

◄**ELLESMERE**
The Mere c1965 E180135

Once upon a time there was an old lady, so the story goes, who lived here, and from whose well could be drawn the finest water. When other wells ran dry, the other villagers came to the old lady and asked if they could take water from her well, but she refused. The spirit of the well heard the old lady's refusal, and was so appalled by this that she made the waters from the well rise up and up. So much water came gushing to the surface that the old lady was drowned and the Mere was formed!

◄ **ELLESMERE**
*Ellesmere
House c1960*
E180118

Ellesmere House is
beautifully sited
just above the
main road and
overlooking the
Mere. The building
is now used as a
residential home.
Between the house
and the lake we
can just see part of
the Cremorne
Gardens, on the
west bank of the
mere, which were
presented to the
townspeople by
Lord Brownlow as
recently as 1953.

▲ **ELLESMERE,** *The Canal c1960* E180122

Now known as the Shropshire Union Canal, the Ellesmere Canal was built at the turn of the 18th
and 19th centuries. The system linked the River Dee with the Mersey, the Trent and the Severn.
It was also intended that there should be a canal going from Ellesmere directly to the north to
reach the sea at Ellesmere Port.

◄ **WHITCHURCH**
Green End c1955
W84050

There has been a
settlement here since
Roman times - their
town was called Mediolanum,
meaning 'the place in the
middle of the plain.' Its
present name was
acquired when the first
stone church (perhaps it
was also whitewashed)
was built by the Normans.

WHITCHURCH
High Street c1950
W84015

This view is dominated by the tower of St Alkmund's church. St Alkmund was a prince of Northumbria, who died in the battle of Worcester in AD 822. In all of England only three churches were dedicated to him, and two of them are in Shropshire. The building second from the right is the former Town Hall, which was built in 1874 and demolished in 1970.

► **WHITCHURCH**
High Street c1955
W84047

The timber-framed building on the right is Walker's Bakery. Although the building dates from around 1450, the bakery has been here since the 1800s, and now also occupies the upper floor, where there is a tea shop. The building is decorated by a particularly fine set of painted stained glass windows - we can see them here just above the sign which reads 'Walker Baker'.

◄ **WHITCHURCH**
High Street c1955
W84030

This is a view of the same street looking down the hill. Notice how in this and the other pictures of Whitchurch, the street lights are suspended above the centre of the street. Little has changed in this view except that the traffic can now travel in one direction only, coming up the hill.

▲ **CALVERHALL,** *The Village c1955* C729005

The building on the left is the Old Jack Inn. It was once the tradition here that any traveller passing by could drink his fill for just one penny from a large leather flagon. Perhaps the price of ale rose too high, or perhaps it was just that too many travellers took advantage of this generosity. Whatever the reason, the flagon mysteriously disappeared in the 1800s!

◀**WOORE**
Main Road c1965
W426002

Although just in Shropshire, Woore seems more closely linked to Staffordshire than Shropshire. In fact, the name Woore (which has also sometimes been spelt as Oure and Owre) means 'a border'. The church, beyond the car park, is described by Nikolaus Pevsner as 'quite individual' - it was built in 1830, and looks rather out of place in an English country village.

MARKET DRAYTON
High Street c1955
M32007

The view here has changed considerably in recent years. In this picture we can already see the growth of the congestion that was soon to become a problem in the centre of the town. Consequently, the buildings on the far left were later demolished when the road was widened to ease the flow of traffic through Market Drayton.

▼ MARKET DRAYTON, *Bank Buildings c1955* M32008

Today the National Provincial Bank has been replaced by the Tudor House Hotel, which occupies the same building. Often when we see buildings of this type we automatically refer to them as Tudor (that is, 16th-century). In fact, there was a disastrous fire in the heart of Market Drayton that took place in 1651, and so despite its appearance the building must be later.

► MARKET DRAYTON
Shropshire Street
c1960 M32055

This is a view of the building in M32008 taken from the other direction. In the foreground is a pub called the Sandbrooks Vaults. The building at the end of the street, behind the man with the basket, was one of those demolished in 1964, soon after this picture was taken, along with the buildings indicated in picture M32007. This building was the Shambles or meat market.

◄ **MARKET DRAYTON**
Stafford Street
c1955 M32029

The Star Hotel, the timber-framed building on the right, is thought to date from the 1660s. Today it still houses a pub, now called Jack Hanby's Place. Notice the soldier in uniform walking away from the camera - just outside the town there are military barracks at Tern Hill.

► **MARKET DRAYTON**
The Swimming Pool
c1960 M32023

The open-air swimming pool in Market Drayton was built in the 1930s; it attracted people from a large area around the town, even from as far away at Stoke on Trent. In fact, during Potters Fortnight each summer, when all the factories in Stoke closed down for the annual holiday, the pool was guaranteed to be packed with visitors to the town.

MARKET DRAYTON
The Basin,
The Shropshire Union
Canal c1965 M32074

When this photograph was taken, the canal system was little used. In recent years, however, canals throughout the country have seen a revival as holidaymakers have discovered boating holidays. Betton Mill, the tall building pictured here, has recently been restored, and now caters expressly for the holiday trade with a tea shop, gift store and even a book 'swop-shop' for all the holidaymakers.

MARKET DRAYTON, *The Canal at Tyrley Locks c1955* M32018

Tyrley (pronounced Turley) Locks consists of a flight of five locks south of Market Drayton. Along with coal, the main products that were shipped along this canal were cheese and milk. Whitchurch, Wem and Market Drayton all had important cheese markets - indeed, in the early years of the 20th century, more Cheshire cheese was being produced in Shropshire than in Cheshire.

CHESWARDINE
St Edward's College c1955 C503010

Despite its Tudor style, Cheswardine Hall was built in 1875. In the relatively short time since it was built, the building has had a chequered history. At the time this photograph was taken, it was occupied by a boy's school, hence the title of the photograph. Today, however, it is used as a nursing home.

HODNET, *The Hall c1960* H379031

Showing many similarities in design to Cheswardine Hall (C503010), Hodnet Hall was built in 1870 and is the home of the Heber-Percy family. The gardens, over 60 acres in all, were laid out in the 1920s, and are open to the public. They are, I think, particularly beautiful in the late spring when the rhododendrons, azaleas and bluebell walks are at their best.

▼ **WESTON UNDER REDCASTLE,** *The Church c1955* W559021

St Luke's church dates from 1791, although there was an earlier church on the site - the registers go back to Tudor times. There is a grave in the churchyard of a slave boy who died here some time in the 18th century. Beside the church, by the road, there is a set of stocks, but no-one locally knows when they were last used.

► **WESTON UNDER REDCASTLE**
St Joseph's Church, Hawkstone Hall c1955
W559028

The Hawkstone estate was originally bought by Sir Rowland Hill, a draper, who in 1549 became the first Protestant Lord Mayor of London. Today the house is home to the Redemptorists; it is used as a training and recuperation centre for missionaries who work all over the world. St Joseph's church is therefore a very recent addition, and was opened in 1932.

◄ **WESTON UNDER REDCASTLE**
Hawkstone Park, The Lake c1955
W559039

In the 18th century the parklands were landscaped with a series of follies, which are now open to the public each summer. As part of this landscaping, the lake we see here was created - the labour force was made up of prisoners of war from the Peninsular War. The park was used again to house prisoners of war during the Second World War.

► **PREES**
Shrewsbury Street c1960 P284001

Prees is a small village that sits beside the road linking Shrewsbury and Whitchurch. Unfortunately, when the bypass was built it actually went right through the village, cutting off the original settlement on the hill with its church from the later roadside settlement. This is the view along the street looking south.

◄ **WEM**
High Street c1955
W457081

Wem is typical of many small country towns serving agricultural communities. In the past it had regular cattle markets and cheese markets, a mill, tanneries and a brewery, but these have now all gone. However, it does have an annual sweet pea festival - the modern hybrid sweet pea was developed here by Henry Eckford in the 1880s.

◀ **PREES**
*Whitchurch
Road c1960*
P284008

It was in Prees that another Rowland Hill was born - this time a soldier. Making his name during the Peninsular War, he then fought (along with four of his brothers) at the Battle of Waterloo. Lord Rowland Hill was nicknamed 'Daddy' by his men because they knew they could trust him to take care of their families should they be wounded or killed in battle.

▲ **WEM,** *High Street c1965* W457040

There was a terrible fire in Wem in 1677, so most of the buildings in the town date from the 1700s or afterwards. One of the few earlier buildings is Dial Cottage, seen here on the right. The building just beyond, Grove End House is a listed building, but it is currently in a state of severe dilapidation and desperately needs rescuing.

◀ **SHAWBURY**
Church Street c1955
S572002

The delightful cottage on the right is one of the relatively few timber-framed houses in Shropshire with a thatched roof. Beyond it is the church of St Mary's. Dating from Norman times, it has a fine carved Norman doorway on the far side. Today Shawbury is best known for its RAF base, which was established in 1916 for what was then called the Royal Flying Corps.

THE WREKIN AND THE INDUSTRIAL EAST

NEWPORT, *The Church c1960* N26027

St Nicholas's church was named for the patron saint of fishermen. Much of the land locally was very marshy until it was drained in the 18th and 19th centuries, and the numerous pools around the town provided fish for the local people with a large surplus for sale. The town's crest therefore includes three fishes as a reminder of the origins of its wealth.

NEWPORT
*St Mary's Street
c1955* N26003

Despite the fact that it is named for a different saint, St Mary's Street can be found just behind the church of St Nicholas. Notice the cobbles - these still survive today, ensuring that the street retains a great deal of its old charm. The sign on the left is another reminder of older trades - it advertises a saddler and harness maker.

NEWPORT, *High Street c1960* N26014

Notice how the High Street widens considerably as it approaches the church. This area, now occupied by buildings, would originally have been used for an open market when the new market was established here in Henry I's reign - Newport means 'new market'. The building in front of the church has since been replaced by a monstrosity that should never have been passed by the local planners.

NEWPORT
High Street c1960
N26023

The planners here have also replaced a number of the buildings along the north side of the High Street. Nikolaus Pevsner's comment about Newport that 'From the point of view of townscape there is nothing better in North Shropshire than Newport' no longer rings true. Fortunately, the buildings on the southern side of the street (seen on the left in picture number N26014) still survive.

EDGMOND
The Village c1955
E23018

Notice the drinking fountain (left) beside the road junction. It was built in 1900, and written across it are the words 'Waste not, want not.' The house behind is rather older; the date 1670 can still be seen on the building, hidden behind the telegraph pole in this picture. Charlotte Sophia Burne lived in the village for a time - she wrote a book on Shropshire folklore which was published in 1881.

EDGMOND, *The Harper Adams Agricultural College c1955* E23004

Today Edgmond is best known for its agricultural college, now known as the Harper Adams University College. It was founded just over 100 years ago thanks to a bequest of £45,496 from a gentleman farmer named Thomas Harper Adams, who died in 1892. In 1926 the college also became the home for the National Institute of Poultry Husbandry.

LILLESHALL
The Abbey c1960
L46030

Following its dissolution in the 16th century, Lilleshall Abbey has become a ruin - its stones were used for the building of many houses in the area. Today it sits abandoned, except for one ghostly monk who can sometimes be seen praying where the altar once stood. The pond in the foreground is a reminder of the importance of fish production locally.

LILLESHALL, *The Hill c1960* L46028

The monument on the hill was erected by the local people in 1836 in memory of their landlord, George Granville Leveson-Gower, Duke of Sutherland. They had reason to be grateful - the duke had been instrumental in introducing modern farming methods on his estate, and had also built decent cottages for his workers. Originally there were four lions guarding the base of the monument, but a lightning strike in 1839 sent them crashing into the gardens of the houses below, and they were never replaced.

► **LILLESHAL**
The National Recreation Centre, The North Front c1955 L46008

Built in 1829 for the Duke of Sutherland, Lilleshall Hall was designed by Sir John Wyattville. In June 1951 it was officially opened by Princess Elizabeth to serve as a National Recreation Centre (at that time serving just the north of England), running courses for a wide range of sports including cricket, archery, athletics, fencing, judo, weightlifting, soccer, netball and tennis.

◄ **LILLESHALL**
The Italian Gardens and The Lawns c1955 L46001

The estate was sold after the First World War, and then used for a time as a pleasure park. One of its advertising slogans invited people to 'see Lilleshall and know the thrill of living'! The garden pictured here is known as Duchess Harriet's ornamental garden, and looks very much the same today. Notice the arches of a Grecian temple folly on the far right. During the Second World War the girls from Cheltenham Ladies' College were evacuated here, and then for a short time it was used as an orphanage for Dr Barnardo's.

▲ **TRENCH,** *Trench Road c1965* T344001

Trench is typical of the many small villages in this part of Shropshire that were combined to form the new town of Telford. Developing as an industrial town in the 18th and 19th centuries and with most of its population employed in mining coal, this road, linking Wellington and Newport, was then lined with miner's cottages. The road has since been replaced with a parallel road nearby.

◄**TRENCH**
Mill Way c1965 T344010

With the announcement of the foundation of the new town of Telford, the developers moved in; today's town is covered with numerous estates just like this one. Notice that the name of the road, Mill Way, is a reminder of the industrial past of the area.

TRENCH
Wrockwardine Wood Church of England Junior School c1965
T344005

A new town means a sudden growth of population as people come to the area seeking work. It therefore follows that the population of such towns generally has a younger average age than the norm, and these young families need schools for their children. This school's architecture is typical of the many schools founded in Telford at around this time.

▼ **OAKENGATES,** *c1960* O1030

This photograph and O1033 are particularly interesting because they were taken not long before work began on the construction of the new town of Telford. Today it would be virtually impossible to compare these views because the whole area has been totally redesigned and built over in the intervening 40 years.

► **OAKENGATES**
c1960 O1033

Notice the spoil heap on the right-hand side of the photograph. There were dozens of these all over the area of the new town, which made it very unsightly at the time when the photograph was taken. Since then, however, they have all been either removed or landscaped, providing pleasant green areas and parkland in the midst of the new town.

◀ **OAKENGATES**
The Square c1965
O1043

The group of buildings with the clock have all gone to make way for a road system around Oakengates. Notice also the little white building on the right next door to George Orme. This was the shop of S A George, whose advertisement painted on the wall tells us that he offered an unusual assortment of services: he was a hairdresser who also sold tobacco, fishing tackle and toys.

▶ **OAKENGATES**
Market Street c1955
O1019

In order to compare this picture with picture number O1044, look for the gable end with the two chimneys as a point of reference. The buildings immediately in front of it have all been replaced. Those in the foreground do survive, however, and now include a computer shop and an Indian restaurant - something that the people here could never have imagined in the 1950s.

OAKENGATES
Market Street c1965
O1044

It is sad that with the development of a large shopping centre in Telford town centre, Oakengates no longer attracts shoppers as it once did - even the branch of Woolworth we see here has since gone. However, Oakengates has another special attraction today - behind these buildings the Oakengates Theatre has been established, and it has built up an excellent reputation for both the quality and variety of its programmes.

OAKENGATES
Oxford Street c1965
O1042

The sign on the left of the picture indicates a free car park. The new town of Telford was built for a population of car owners, so that until recently, Telford was very proud to advertise the presence in the town of over 3,000 free parking places. Much to the disgust of local people parking charges have now been introduced.

◄**WELLINGTON**
The Green c1965
W44083

This is the view from the church. There are few graves here, although headstones hidden amongst the shrubs on the left remind churchgoers that this was once a graveyard too. Today the flower beds have also gone, and the whole area is under grass. The white building in the centre is the office of Barber & Son, a local estate agents founded in 1848.

◄ **WELLINGTON**
The Parish Church c1960
W44049

The car in front of the church door is decorated with ribbons, and a group of photographers is waiting nearby -a wedding must be taking place. The church is All Saints', and was designed in 1790 by George Steuart, an architect responsible for many important buildings in Shropshire. A former curate at the church was Patrick Bronte, father of Charlotte, Emily, Anne and Branwell.

▲ **WELLINGTON,** *Church Street c1965* W44050

Shropshire has traditionally been a supporter of the Conservative party. This was to change, however, with the development of the new town, and the people here have been strong Labour supporters for some years now. When the photograph is enlarged, however, a banner on one of the buildings in the distance can be seen to read 'Conservative Campaign HQ. Hold onto a good MP.' The tall Victorian building is Barclays Bank. Today Barclays still occupies the same site, but in a 1960s monstrosity of a building - how it was ever approved by the planners beats me.

◄ **WELLINGTON**
Holyhead Road and Mill Bank c1965
W44074

This road junction is just to the south of the centre of Wellington, and sits astride the London to Holyhead road that was built by Thomas Telford in the early 1800s. Telford was the County Surveyor for Shropshire at the time, and was associated with the building of roads and also of bridges, canals and aqueducts, to name just a few of his projects.

WELLINGTON
Market Square c1965
W44080

It was in one of the houses here that William Withering was born in 1741. A member of the Lunar Society (other members included the likes of Erasmus Darwin, Josiah Wedgwood, Matthew Boulton, James Watt and Joseph Priestley - all great scientific names of 18th-century England), he discovered the medicinal properties of digitalis (from foxgloves) for the treatment of heart conditions.

▶ **THE WREKIN**
The Needle's Eye
c1960 W152057

The Wrekin is a large hill in the centre of Shropshire dominating both Shrewsbury and Telford. The Needle's Eye is the name given to the split in the rock shown here - it is said to have been formed when two giants had a fight. One giant threw his spade at the other. The spade missed its target, but instead slashed into the hillside.

◀ **THE WREKIN** *c1960*
W152095

Although this is not the highest point in the county, the view from the top of the hill is superb in all directions. Our Iron Age ancestors appreciated the importance of the site and built a hill fort on the top, but it was abandoned when the Romans conquered the region. Today it is occupied by tall communication masts.

▲ **THE WREKIN,** *The Forest Glen Pavilion c1955* W152040

The Wrekin has attracted keen walkers for years, and many people would have welcomed a cup of tea served here. The Pavilion has gone now, but not completely. The building was dismantled and re-erected in the Blist's Hill Museum in Ironbridge, and so people are still being served with cups of tea within its walls.

◄**BUILDWAS**
The Bridge c1955
B244006

The earliest bridge on this site was built by the monks of nearby Buildwas Abbey. It was destroyed in a great flood in 1795, and was replaced by a cast iron bridge built by Thomas Telford. The bridge we see here was then built in 1905 to replace Telford's bridge; it has itself since been replaced by a fourth bridge built on this site in 1992.

► **IRONBRIDGE**
c1960 I20055

Of course, this name only dates from the time after the bridge was built in 1779. Before then, the area was simply part of the borough of Madeley, just to the north. The church we see here, St Luke's, was designed by Thomas Smith of Madeley and built in 1836 - by that time a large population had settled here, and required a church to serve their needs.

◄ **IRONBRIDGE**
The Bridge c1955
I20033

Building the world's first iron bridge was an expensive venture for Abraham Darby III. The idea was first proposed by the Shropshire architect, Thomas Farnolls Pritchard, and a consortium was founded to finance it. In fact, when he died Darby was still paying off the debts that he had accrued from building it. A toll bridge, it opened to the public on 1 January 1781.

▲ **IRONBRIDGE,** *Tontine Hill c1955* 120035

The road is named after the Tontine Hotel, which was built in 1783 to accommodate visitors coming to see the new bridge. The name refers to a form of investment: as investors in the company (in this case the hotel) died, their assets were passed to the surviving investors. This gave the business more chance of survival with only one owner at the end.

◀**IRONBRIDGE**
Dale Road c1960 120058

This is the main road that links Ironbridge with Coalbrookdale, the place where the Industrial Revolution really did start in 1709 when Abraham Darby I discovered a method of smelting iron ore using coke as opposed to charcoal. Rose Cottage (right) is therefore one of the few buildings in the area to predate the Industrial Revolution - it has recently been restored.

DAWLEY
The Webb Memorial
c1955 D169007

This memorial honours a local son, Matthew Webb, who in 1875 was the first man to swim across the English Channel. Webb was born near here in 1848 and learnt to swim in the River Severn, where currents can be treacherous. The memorial was unveiled in 1909, and bears a most appropriate inscription - 'Nothing great is easy.'

MADELEY, *The Old Court House c1950* M4004

Now a hotel, the Old Court House was built by Sir Robert Brooke - he had bought the estate for £946 (an enormous sum of money for the times) following the dissolution of the monasteries by Henry VIII. The name of the house comes about because he was a lawyer and also speaker of the House of Commons.

MADELEY, *St Michael's Church c1955* M4013

This most unusual octagonal church is one of three churches in Shropshire that were built by Thomas Telford. This one dates from 1796. Earlier in the 18th century John Fletcher, a close friend of the famous Methodist, John Wesley, served here as vicar. His cast iron tomb sits in the church yard.

SHIFNAL
Market Place c1955
S117009

There was a terrible fire in the town in 1591, so all the timber buildings in the town date from afterwards. Generally when buildings are restored, the plasterwork is often removed to reveal the old timber beneath; however, on the Star Hotel on the far left of the picture, the timber work has since been plastered over.

▼ **SHIFNAL**
Church Street c1955 S117011

Shifnal is typical of many towns where the focus of the town appears to have shifted following the arrival of the railways. Once, St Andrew's church would have been in the heart of the town; now it sits quietly to one side, and the main market area has grown closer to the railway station. A number of the buildings we see here have since been demolished.

► **SHIFNAL**
Market Place c1955
S117023

We are looking north. The railway bridge that crosses over Market Place is a terrible eyesore to this day. Notice the parked delivery van - the writing on it advertises Morris & Co Ltd. Morris's grocery company was founded in 1856 in Shrewsbury. The company soon had an excellent reputation for the quality of its merchandise, so that before long they were delivering goods all around the county.

◄ **SHIFNAL**
The Broadway
c1965 S117027

Despite the growth of
Shifnal (it developed
to provide
accommodation for
both Birmingham and
Wolverhampton to the
east and the new town
of Telford to the west),
it has managed to
retain much of its
charm and
individuality.
Unfortunately, not
everything has
survived - the toll
house (centre right)
was removed when
the road was widened.

► **TONG**
St Bartholemew's Church
c1955 T56001

This is a particularly beautiful
church, which has come to be
known as the 'Westminster of the
Midlands'; it has a fan-vaulted
'Golden Chapel' and superb
alabaster tombs and carved
misericords. The church is perhaps
better known, however, as the place
where Little Nell was buried in
Charles Dickens' book 'The Old
Curiosity Shop'. Then, as now,
people flocked to visit places where
fictional stories took place, and an
enterprising churchwarden
dedicated an old grave to Little Nell
for visitors to see. He even forged an
entry in the church's burial register.

TONG
Church Farm c1955
T56004

The sign by the roadside advertises the sale of cream, milk and eggs for passers-by, among other things. Notice also the three churns of milk awaiting collection in front of the entrance to the farm. Today the farm is home to the Tong Riding School.

ALBRIGHTON, *The Shrewsbury Arms Hotel c1965* A24076

It has been suggested that the Shrewsbury Arms is so called because it once belonged to the Earls of Shrewsbury. The church of St Mary Magdalene sits across the road. Studying photographs in the Francis Frith collection, one is struck by how often buildings that were once easy to see are now obscured by trees. Here the opposite has happened - the trees have been removed.

ALBRIGHTON
High Street c1965
A24075

This is another town that now serves largely as a dormitory town to both Birmingham and the Black Country, and also to the new town of Telford. Many of the people here also work at the nearby Cosford RAF base; Cosford is the home of the Aerospace Museum with its collection of missiles, warplanes, retired passenger aircraft and aero engines.

RYTON, *The Village c1960* R79020

Hardly a village, Ryton would be better described as a small hamlet hidden amongst the hills on the banks of the River Worfe. The river twists and turns through the hills, and the name Worfe means 'winding river'.

◄**BECKBURY**
The Village c1965
B864008

Michael Raven in his book on Shropshire says of Beckbury that 'the council has spoiled the village with its bland, red brick council houses.' Judging from the buildings shown here, we can see exactly what he means.

◄ **BECKBURY**
The Seven Stars Inn c1965
B864003

Beckbury, just a mile or so to the south, can certainly be described as a village, and it still retains its pub, the Seven Stars. A local man called Square Stubbs was born in Beckbury in 1671 - he used to ride up to 20 miles every day, always at a steady trot that became known as 'Stubbs' pace'.

▲ **BROSELEY,** *The Square c1965* B234017

Broseley was once the only sizeable town in what is now known as the Ironbridge Gorge area. It was an important industrial centre, and coal was mined and shipped from here down the River Severn. Bricks were also produced locally, and clay was used to make china, tiles and clay pipes. Today there is an excellent clay pipe museum in the town.

◄ **BROSELEY**
Willey Old Hall c1960
B234015

The area around Willey Old Hall seems a million miles away from industry, yet there were once iron forges all around. One forge owner was John Wilkinson, otherwise known as 'Ironmad' Wilkinson. It was near here that, to the great amusement of most of the local populace, he built an iron boat. It was launched on the River Severn in 1787, and another milestone in industrial development was reached. This photograph shows the stable block of the old hall, now converted into private houses.

▶ **BRIDGNORTH**
Stoneway Steps c1960 B204098

The town of Bridgnorth is divided between High Town on the hilltop and Low Town beside the river. A number of staircases link the two - the Stoneway Steps, shown here, has 178 steps to climb. The iron buttress holding the brick walls apart is known as Pope's Spectacles, named after a man called John Pope who ran the foundry in the town where it was made.

▼ **BRIDGNORTH**
The Bridge c1950 B204009

The first bridge, the one that gave the town its name, was built long ago. This bridge, however, was built in 1823; it has been described as a 'mongrel structure', because it is thought to incorporate parts of an earlier 14th-century structure within it. The earlier bridge had a chapel on it where travellers could stop and pray for a safe journey as they set off.

▶ **BRIDGNORTH**
The Town Hall and the High Street c1950
B204061

The Town Hall in the centre of the street makes the movement of traffic very difficult along here, and I always feel that it is a minor miracle that the 1960s town planners allowed it to survive. Fortunately it still stands here, so that traffic is now one-way, going around it on the right-hand side.

◄ **BRIDGNORTH**
The Cable Lift
c1965 B204145

An easier way to get from one part of town to the other would be to take the cable car. It was opened in 1892, when a ticket up or down cost 1d (one old penny). Today only return tickets are available, and these now cost 70 pence.

BRIDGNORTH
Baxter's House c1960
B204105

The little timber-framed cottage has an inscription that tells us it was the home of Richard Baxter in the years 1640-41. Baxter was a non-conformist religious thinker, and was later to become a well-loved preacher in nearby Kidderminster. However, he once described the people of Bridgnorth, not very kindly, as 'ignorant and dead hearted'!

▶ **WORFIELD**
The Village c1960 W427002

This view looks out over the village of Worfield from St Peter's church, a very large church for such a small village, which really consists of just the one street. Although the village may be small, the parish served by the church covered an area of some 20 square miles.

▼ **QUATFORD**
The Church c1960 Q13025

Legend has it that this church was founded by Adeliza, the wife of Roger de Montgomery. Montgomery had come to England with William the Conqueror, and had been given control of Shropshire. When his wife travelled across the Channel to join him, there was a terrible storm. Terrified, Adeliza prayed to God that should she safely complete her journey, she would build a church at the place where she met her husband. She met her husband under a nearby oak tree (which still survives!) and then built the first church on this site.

▶ **QUATFORD**
The Severn Valley Café c1965 Q13011

The Severn Valley Café still survives, although now it is a Little Chef restaurant serving people travelling along the road between Bridgnorth and Kidderminster. It certainly has a magnificent site right on top of a cliff with excellent views over the River Severn beyond.

◄**QUATFORD**
The Severn Valley Caravan Park
c1965 Q13017

Just behind and some way below the Little Chef, this caravan park sits beside the River Severn. At first glance it would appear that caravan designs have changed less in the last 40 years than they had in the previous ten - many of these look remarkably modern. The small chalets look very dated today, however, yet many of them still survive.

THE SOUTH SHROPSHIRE HILLS AND LUDLOW

MUCH WENLOCK
Wenlock Priory c1955 M104082

Wenlock Priory was dissolved in the 16th century, and much of the stone was probably taken to build farms and houses in the locality. Much fine carving detail does survive. The stone structure in the foreground is a medieval wash-basin with delightful carvings of the saints on it. Notice also the topiary, which is now much more impressive than it was in this photograph.

MUCH WENLOCK, *The Bull Ring c1960* M104138

Much Wenlock is the most delightfully evocative town, so much so that Ellis Peters (the local author of the Brother Cadfael detective books set in the 12th century) once said of the town that you almost expect a shopper in the newsagents here to ask for a copy of the Anglo-Saxon Chronicle.

◄ **COUND**
The Village c1950
C718003

The village of Cound is split in two by the Coundmoor Brook - this photograph was taken in Upper Cound, which is separated from the earlier part of the village (where the church stands). Despite their appearance, both the timber buildings shown here date from the early 1900s.

◄MUCH WENLOCK
High Street
c1965 M104146

Although the exterior of Barclays Bank only goes back to the 17th century, there are timbers within the building that date to 1408. Similarly, Reynald's Mansion, on the right, has a date on the façade of 1682 - but this is only the date when it was given a 'facelift'. The core of the building was also erected in the early 1400s.

▲ **COUND,** *The Village c1950* C718008

The timber building shown here is much older than the ones in C718003. Crossing the river near the village there was once an iron bridge, built by Thomas Telford in 1818. It became too weak for modern traffic, and was removed in the 1960s with the intention that it should become an ornamental bridge at Attingham Park. Instead it now serves as a footbridge in Telford's town centre.

◄ACTON BURNELL
The Castle c1960 A363002

The castle at Acton Burnell was built at the end of the 13th century by Robert Burnell, Bishop of Bath and Wells and Lord Chancellor of England. It is thought that the first proper meeting of Parliament, called by the members themselves rather than at the behest of the King, was held in a barn just next to the castle. There were obviously many merchants amongst the members, as the first statute passed agreed that debtors should accept, when taking a loan, that they must pay their debts within a set time.

CARDINGTON
The Village c1960
C763014

This is a beautiful example of the mixing of stone and timberwork that is typical of many houses that snuggle amongst the hills of southern Shropshire. The house is called Brook House; there is an inscription above the crest over the porch (just to the right of the road sign) that dates the building to 1574.

SHIPTON, *The Hall c1960* S837009

Built in 1587, Shipton Hall was a wedding present from Richard Lutwyche to his daughter, Elizabeth, when she married Thomas Mytton. Another Elizabeth, the Queen, stayed here soon afterwards. She was visiting Ludlow at the time, and went out riding in the countryside nearby with a large party of retainers; she was caught in a storm, and sought shelter here for the night.

LONGVILLE IN THE DALE, *The YHA Hostel, Main Hall c1960* L357017

The youth hostel occupies Wilderhope Manor, which was built in 1586. It was bought by John Cadbury (of Cadbury's Chocolate), who later presented it to the National Trust. Notice the beautiful plasterwork on the ceiling of the dining hall. During the time of the Civil War the house was owned by Major Thomas Smallman, who was a supporter of the Royalists.

LONGVILLE IN THE DALE, *The YHA Hostel, Caer Caradoc Room c1960* L357008

Would such spartan conditions be acceptable to youth hostellers today? Today's guests can be assured of a good night's sleep - unless they are disturbed by the ghost of Major Smallman. He was once pursued by Parliamentarians along Wenlock Edge. To escape, he forced his horse to jump over the precipice - the horse was killed, but Smallman survived. The place where he jumped is still known as Major's Leap.

CHURCH STRETTON
c1965 C104186

The early Anglo-Saxon settlement of Church Stretton sat, despite its name, which means 'the settlement on the street', a little distance away from the Roman road of Watling Street. Today the town spreads over both sides of the ancient highway. Here we see St Lawrence's church, the earliest part of which dates from the 12th century.

CHURCH STRETTON, *High Street c1965* C104189

The lady on the left is probably reading the notices for forthcoming attractions in the Silvester Horne Institute, which is just behind the trees. The hall is still used today for many society meetings. Across the road, George Dakin's grocery store is now known as the Oriental Cottage, and serves Chinese food.

▶ **CHURCH STRETTON**
Tudor Cottage, High Street c1965
C104188

This old cottage has had a remarkable transformation in recent years. The timber work on the gable end of the building fronting the road remains the same, but the front wall is now all stone, giving the entire structure a much more medieval appearance.

◀ **CHURCH STRETTON**
The Longmynd Hotel c1965 C104206

It was in Victorian times that Stretton became popular with visitors, following the building of the railway line. The Longmynd Hotel has a superb site half-way up the hill with wonderful views towards the south. It is still a family-run hotel; it is particularly popular with walkers, who use it as a base from which to explore the Shropshire hills.

▲ **CHURCH STRETTON,** *The Denehurst Hotel c1955* C104131

Apparently Church Stretton was especially popular with people who had previously worked in India and found the area 'similar to Simla' - such people retired here in their droves. The Denehurst Hotel has recently been demolished, and the site is currently being used for the building of new retirement apartments - this is evidently still a popular area to retire to!

◀ **LITTLE STRETTON**
*All Saints' Church
c1955* L59095

Despite its timber frame and 'olde worlde' appearance, this is a relatively new church. It was built in 1903 by Alice Elizabeth Gibbon. She died in 1932, and has a memorial inside the building. Internally, as well as externally, the church has obviously been heavily influenced in its style by the Arts and Crafts movement that was very much in fashion at the time.

LITTLE STRETTON
The Ancient House
c1955 L59094

There are three Strettons in Shropshire, all running into each other. Legend has it that the King once visited and admired the first little village he came to, and it became Little Stretton. At the next he admired the fine church - hence Church Stretton. When he came to the third Stretton, he remarked: 'But they're all called Stretton!' and so it became known as All Stretton.

CHURCH STRETTON, *The Chalet Pavilion and The Old Carding Mill Café c1965* C104170

Much of the Long Mynd is now managed by the National Trust. Although there have evidently been some changes in the intervening years, these buildings still provide visitors to the area with food and drink, not to mention leaflets on local walks and souvenirs for the discerning buyer.

CHURCH STRETTON
Carding Mill Valley c1965 C104199

Carding Mill Valley is so called because it was here that wool shorn from the local sheep was carded - in other words, it was combed before being spun into thread. Today it is a popular starting point for many people walking up onto the hills, and the car park we see here can be packed with cars on a summer's day.

THE LONG MYND, *Near the Devil's Mouth c1960* T356005

There used to be a fair in Church Stretton every November. If the weather turned bad during the fair, many people who then tried to walk home over the hills were killed, so that it came to be known as the Dead Man's Fair. These hills can be treacherous, and many local names reflect this; another valley, for example, is called Dead Man's Hollow.

▼ **CHIRBURY**, *The Village c1950* C504010

Overlooking Chirbury is the church of St Michael. It gives one a strange feeling to stand inside the church, because the main walls of the nave have a definite lean outwards. There is a line of buttresses against the outside walls that hold the entire structure up. It is to be hoped that these will continue to keep the church standing for another 700 years and more.

► **CHIRBURY**
The Hotel and the Lych Gate c1950 C504007

The building on the left, now without its cover of ivy, is the Herbert Arms. One member of the family was Lord Herbert, an historian, philosopher and diplomat in the 16th century. He had an extensive (and now extremely valuable) chained library of books, which he left to the villagers. It was stored for many years in the local schoolhouse, but it is now kept in Shrewsbury.

◄ **BISHOP'S CASTLE**
High Street c1955
B621017

This view shows the High Street dominated, at the top of the hill, by the Town Hall. Today the town has a wonderfully avant garde feel about it; it has some very original shops, including The Awareness Shop - 'a spiritual store for seekers.' The shop with the bow window near the centre of the photograph is Naiad's Well, and is run by a witch who sells her spells and gives courses in witchcraft. The appearance of such a shop was a bit much, even for the people of Bishop's Castle, and so she now has a sign in her window inviting anyone who is concerned about her services to call in and have a chat.

► **LYDBURY NORTH**
The Church c1960
L219002

Like many other local churches, St Michael's has a strong, almost military, look about its tower. This was wild border country, and the towers of these churches served as lookouts for possible marauding Welshmen! It is just possible to make out the clock face on the church tower - it is most unusual as it only has one hand to tell the hour of the day.

◄ **NEWCASTLE**
The Crown Inn c1960
N152017

Small communities in remote rural areas have suffered considerably in recent years. First local schools have closed, and then shops, post offices and pubs have followed suit. Sometimes the only way to retain these facilities has been to combine them under one roof. Today the Crown Inn has an extension at the far end, the Crown Shop.

◄LYDBURY NORTH
Walcot Hall
c1960 L219003

Walcot Hall was built by Sir William Chambers in 1763 for Robert Clive, Clive of India. Clive's greatest victory in India was at the battle of Plassey. To commemorate this, he planted trees on the estate to spell out the word 'Plassey'. Unfortunately, these proved to be such a good landmark that they were cut down during the Second World War for fear that they might help guide Luftwaffe pilots.

▲ **CLUN,** *The View from the Mowdens c1960* C507003

We can see the village of Clun in the valley, with the keep of its old castle standing guard. Actually this castle was less a military stronghold than a centre for hunting. In medieval times, the Mowdens and the surrounding district were all part of Clun Forest, and subject to Forest Law in much the same way as the New Forest in the south of England.

◄CLUN
Church Street c1950
C507010

Although it only has a small population, Clun is always referred to as a town rather than a village. Its layout is extremely elongated, with the castle and market area at one end and the church (with presumably the original settlement site) up on the hill on the other side of the valley.

▼ **CLUN,** *The View from Church Bank c1960* C507015

The name Clun simply means 'church'. Since this word comes from the old British language (in Welsh it has developed into 'llan'), it implies that there was a Christian community here long before the Anglo-Saxons invaded and were themselves converted. Here we see the church of St George on its ancient hilltop site overlooking the town that has developed in the valley below.

▶ **CLUN**
The Old Bridge c1960 C507053

Crossing the River Clun in the valley is the most delightful medieval bridge, which we can see here just beyond the white van. It was built in around 1450, and can cause real problems for modern large coaches and articulated trucks. Alternative routes are very, very much longer! The barn on the left of the photograph has since been removed, and this area beside the river is now a car park for visitors to the nearby castle. The building beside the bridge, now called Bridge Crafts, houses a post office, craft centre and tea shop.

◄ CRAVEN ARMS
Market Street
c1955 C539005

This is a view of the street looking south. The shop on the right is a branch of W H Smith, with the old style of sign standing proud from the wall - some of these still survive on a few branches around the country. Notice how similar the shop front is to the one in Wellington, shown in picture number W44080.

► CRAVEN ARMS
The Stokesay Castle Hotel c1955 C539001

Now known as the Stokesay Castle Inn, this hotel overlooks a new tourist attraction in the town - a museum of the Shropshire countryside. In the past many of the visitors to the area would have come in order to enjoy country pursuits, and it is interesting to see the round sign on the hotel wall for members of the Cyclists Touring Club.

CRAVEN ARMS
Market Street c1955
C539004

Despite its name, there are very few shops in Market Street today. Notice, particularly, the young man in the white coat who is standing on the pavement smiling at the Frith photographer - he is probably a shop assistant in the greengrocer's shop behind him. This building has now gone, and has been replaced by one that sits further back, off the street.

▼ **STOKESAY,** *The Castle c1955* S202001

Undoubtedly this is one of the most romantic medieval sites in all of England. Dating from the end of the 13th century, technically it is not a castle at all, but a moated manor house, and it would have been very open to attack. Knowing this, the occupants during the Civil War wisely abandoned the castle, so that only its walls and original gatehouse were then demolished.

► **LUDLOW**
Dinham Bridge and the Castle c1955 L111018

Ludlow, today, is an epicure's delight - between them, the restaurants of this small town in the Welsh borders have acquired more Michelin stars than any other town in the country apart from London. One of the restaurants can be found amongst the group of buildings just beside Dinham Bridge, under the hill on which Ludlow Castle stands.

◄ **LUDLOW**
The Broad Gate
c1955 L111065

A misnomer if ever there was one, Broad Gate is the last surviving gate in Ludlow's medieval town walls. It is the broad streets on either side that give the gate its name. The Wheatsheaf pub is haunted by a mischievous ghost who pinches the bottoms of ladies whom he fancies. Mind you, it does give any 'gentleman' who wants to pinch a lady's bottom a ready-made excuse!

► **LUDLOW**
Broad Street c1955
L111040

The timber framed building in the foreground is the former Angel Hotel, an important coaching inn in the 18th and 19th centuries. It was recently sold, and has since been converted into a number of separate apartments.

LUDLOW, *The Butter Cross c1960* L111090

Completed in 1746, the Butter Cross cost nearly £1,000, and was designed by William Baker, a 'gentleman-farmer' from Audlem in Cheshire. The ground floor was a market, and the upper floor was then a charity school for 45 children. Apparently by 1830 there were 170 boys enrolled at the school. Around the time this photograph was taken, it housed 'the best local museum in Britain.'

TITTERSTONE
Clee Hill, c1955 T338014

Standing 533 metres (1,750ft) above sea level, the hill is made up of a stone known as dhustone (from the Welsh word 'dhu', meaning 'black'). The deep scarring resulting from extensive quarrying over the years can clearly be seen in the picture. Today, however, there is another landmark on the hilltop - a radar 'golf ball' built during the Cold War to watch Russian aircraft movements.

CLEE HILL, *The Village c1955* C505025

If there is any breeze blowing, it will blow onto Clee Hill, and consequently the village can sometimes be very bleak. One of the pubs in the village is called the Kremlin - most appropriate in a cold winter. The main shop in the town is the one beyond the parked cars - then a branch of the Co-op, it is now a combined store and post office

CLEE HILL
The Village c1955
C505030

The shop on the right, a bakery, has gone, and the whole building is now a private house. However, there is still a bakery in the village - it has simply moved to the building next door. Above the roofs of the buildings beyond we can see the spire of St Peter's church, which has since been removed.

CLEE HILL *c1960* C505056

This remote barren countryside would seem to be very uninviting. However, people have always lived here, and the hillside is covered with the remains of bell pits - ancient open-cast mines where people have dug for coal from the 13th century. This view shows the main road that links Ludlow with Cleobury Mortimer - it is a spectacular drive, with wonderful views to the south.

CLEOBURY MORTIMER
c1960 C506029

Cleobury, pronounced Clibbery, was once a stronghold of the powerful Mortimer family; they also owned castles in, for example, Ludlow, Wigmore and Chirk. One member of the family even became King of England - Edward IV. The town also claims to be the birthplace of the 14th-century poet William Langland, although it has to be said that Ledbury and Great Malvern make the same claim.

CLEOBURY MORTIMER, *High Street c1955* C506032

This is the view as one comes into the town from the west. The road on the right, Vaughan Road, now leads into an estate with a number of new houses. Otherwise, although the cars are a clue to when the picture was taken, the view looks very much the same today. Notice the slight bend in the line of the steeple in the distance.

▶ **CLEOBURY MORTIMER**
The Talbot Hotel c1955 C506011

In this photograph the kink in the steeple of St Mary's church is very evident. The main body of the steeple is built on a timber frame. Unseasoned timber was used when it was built, and as it has dried out over time, it has warped causing the entire structure to twist slightly. Nikolaus Pevsner describes the church as 'an uncommonly pure building.'

◀ **CLEOBURY MORTIMER**
Church Street c1965
C506070

The Talbot is named for the Earls of Shrewsbury. The first earl was described by Shakespeare as the 'Scourge of France.' He died fighting in France in 1453, and was buried in Rouen with just his heart being brought back for burial in Shropshire. The rest of his body was later exhumed, and also came home. The sign outside the hotel advertises lunches for 5s (25p).

▲ **CLEOBURY MORTIMER,** *Lower Street c1955* C506018

Although the title of the photograph is Lower Street, we are in fact still on Church Street at this point - the grass on the left of the picture is part of the churchyard for St Mary's.

◄**NASH**
The Court c1965
N222205

This beautiful house, still privately owned, was built in 1760 and is little changed, although the ivy that covers the building here has now been removed.

BURFORD, *The Gardens, the Lake and the Café c1965* B859107

Burford sits right on the county boundary with Herefordshire - the boundary is defined by the River Teme at this point. The café pictured here is now a private house beside the main road to Tenbury Wells. The lake in the foreground is a nature reserve, and it sits within the grounds of Burford House - this is now also the home of the National Clematis Collection.

114

INDEX

Frith Book Co Titles

www.francisfrith.co.uk

The Frith Book Company publishes over 100 new titles each year. A selection of those currently available is listed below. For latest catalogue please contact Frith Book Co.
Town Books 96 pages, approximately 100 photos. **County and Themed Books** 128 pages, approximately 150 photos (unless specified). All titles hardback with laminated case and jacket, except those indicated pb (paperback).

Amersham, Chesham & Rickmansworth (pb)	1-85937-340-2	£9.99	Devon (pb)	1-85937-297-x	£9.99
Andover (pb)	1-85937-292-9	£9.99	Devon Churches (pb)	1-85937-250-3	£9.99
Aylesbury (pb)	1-85937-227-9	£9.99	Dorchester (pb)	1-85937-307-0	£9.99
Barnstaple (pb)	1-85937-300-3	£9.99	Dorset (pb)	1-85937-269-4	£9.99
Basildon Living Memories (pb)	1-85937-515-4	£9.99	Dorset Coast (pb)	1-85937-299-6	£9.99
Bath (pb)	1-85937-419-0	£9.99	Dorset Living Memories (pb)	1-85937-584-7	£9.99
Bedford (pb)	1-85937-205-8	£9.99	Down the Severn (pb)	1-85937-560-x	£9.99
Bedfordshire Living Memories	1-85937-513-8	£14.99	Down The Thames (pb)	1-85937-278-3	£9.99
Belfast (pb)	1-85937-303-8	£9.99	Down the Trent	1-85937-311-9	£14.99
Berkshire (pb)	1-85937-191-4	£9.99	East Anglia (pb)	1-85937-265-1	£9.99
Berkshire Churches	1-85937-170-1	£17.99	East Grinstead (pb)	1-85937-138-8	£9.99
Berkshire Living Memories	1-85937-332-1	£14.99	East London	1-85937-080-2	£14.99
Black Country	1-85937-497-2	£12.99	East Sussex (pb)	1-85937-606-1	£9.99
Blackpool (pb)	1-85937-393-3	£9.99	Eastbourne (pb)	1-85937-399-2	£9.99
Bognor Regis (pb)	1-85937-431-x	£9.99	Edinburgh (pb)	1-85937-193-0	£8.99
Bournemouth (pb)	1-85937-545-6	£9.99	England In The 1880s	1-85937-331-3	£17.99
Bradford (pb)	1-85937-204-x	£9.99	Essex - Second Selection	1-85937-456-5	£14.99
Bridgend (pb)	1-85937-386-0	£7.99	Essex (pb)	1-85937-270-8	£9.99
Bridgwater (pb)	1-85937-305-4	£9.99	Essex Coast	1-85937-342-9	£14.99
Bridport (pb)	1-85937-327-5	£9.99	Essex Living Memories	1-85937-490-5	£14.99
Brighton (pb)	1-85937-192-2	£8.99	Exeter	1-85937-539-1	£9.99
Bristol (pb)	1-85937-264-3	£9.99	Exmoor (pb)	1-85937-608-8	£9.99
British Life A Century Ago (pb)	1-85937-213-9	£9.99	Falmouth (pb)	1-85937-594-4	£9.99
Buckinghamshire (pb)	1-85937-200-7	£9.99	Folkestone (pb)	1-85937-124-8	£9.99
Camberley (pb)	1-85937-222-8	£9.99	Frome (pb)	1-85937-317-8	£9.99
Cambridge (pb)	1-85937-422-0	£9.99	Glamorgan	1-85937-488-3	£14.99
Cambridgeshire (pb)	1-85937-420-4	£9.99	Glasgow (pb)	1-85937-190-6	£9.99
Cambridgeshire Villages	1-85937-523-5	£14.99	Glastonbury (pb)	1-85937-338-0	£7.99
Canals And Waterways (pb)	1-85937-291-0	£9.99	Gloucester (pb)	1-85937-232-5	£9.99
Canterbury Cathedral (pb)	1-85937-179-5	£9.99	Gloucestershire (pb)	1-85937-561-8	£9.99
Cardiff (pb)	1-85937-093-4	£9.99	Great Yarmouth (pb)	1-85937-426-3	£9.99
Carmarthenshire (pb)	1-85937-604-5	£9.99	Greater Manchester (pb)	1-85937-266-x	£9.99
Chelmsford (pb)	1-85937-310-0	£9.99	Guildford (pb)	1-85937-410-7	£9.99
Cheltenham (pb)	1-85937-095-0	£9.99	Hampshire (pb)	1-85937-279-1	£9.99
Cheshire (pb)	1-85937-271-6	£9.99	Harrogate (pb)	1-85937-423-9	£9.99
Chester (pb)	1-85937-382 8	£9.99	Hastings and Bexhill (pb)	1-85937-131-0	£9.99
Chesterfield (pb)	1-85937-378-x	£9.99	Heart of Lancashire (pb)	1-85937-197-3	£9.99
Chichester (pb)	1-85937-228-7	£9.99	Helston (pb)	1-85937-214-7	£9.99
Churches of East Cornwall (pb)	1-85937-249-x	£9.99	Hereford (pb)	1-85937-175-2	£9.99
Churches of Hampshire (pb)	1-85937-207-4	£9.99	Herefordshire (pb)	1-85937-567-7	£9.99
Cinque Ports & Two Ancient Towns	1-85937-492-1	£14.99	Herefordshire Living Memories	1-85937-514-6	£14.99
Colchester (pb)	1-85937-188-4	£8.99	Hertfordshire (pb)	1-85937-247-3	£9.99
Cornwall (pb)	1-85937-229-5	£9.99	Horsham (pb)	1-85937-432-8	£9.99
Cornwall Living Memories	1-85937-248-1	£14.99	Humberside (pb)	1-85937-605-3	£9.99
Cotswolds (pb)	1-85937-230-9	£9.99	Hythe, Romney Marsh, Ashford (pb)	1-85937-256-2	£9.99
Cotswolds Living Memories	1-85937-255-4	£14.99	Ipswich (pb)	1-85937-424-7	£9.99
County Durham (pb)	1-85937-398-4	£9.99	Isle of Man (pb)	1-85937-268-6	£9.99
Croydon Living Memories (pb)	1-85937-162-0	£9.99	Isle of Wight (pb)	1-85937-429-8	£9.99
Cumbria (pb)	1-85937-621-5	£9.99	Isle of Wight Living Memories	1-85937-304-6	£14.99
Derby (pb)	1-85937-367-4	£9.99	Kent (pb)	1-85937-189-2	£9.99
Derbyshire (pb)	1-85937-196-5	£9.99	Kent Living Memories(pb)	1-85937-401-8	£9.99
Derbyshire Living Memories	1-85937-330-5	£14.99	Kings Lynn (pb)	1-85937-334-8	£9.99

Available from your local bookshop or from the publisher

Frith Book Co Titles (continued)

Title	ISBN	Price	Title	ISBN	Price
Lake District (pb)	1-85937-275-9	£9.99	Sherborne (pb)	1-85937-301-1	£9.99
Lancashire Living Memories	1-85937-335-6	£14.99	Shrewsbury (pb)	1-85937-325-9	£9.99
Lancaster, Morecambe, Heysham (pb)	1-85937-233-3	£9.99	Shropshire (pb)	1-85937-326-7	£9.99
Leeds (pb)	1-85937-202-3	£9.99	Shropshire Living Memories	1-85937-643-6	£14.99
Leicester (pb)	1-85937-381-x	£9.99	Somerset	1-85937-153-1	£14.99
Leicestershire & Rutland Living Memories	1-85937-500-6	£12.99	South Devon Coast	1-85937-107-8	£14.99
Leicestershire (pb)	1-85937-185-x	£9.99	South Devon Living Memories (pb)	1-85937-609-6	£9.99
Lighthouses	1-85937-257-0	£9.99	South East London (pb)	1-85937-263-5	£9.99
Lincoln (pb)	1-85937-380-1	£9.99	South Somerset	1-85937-318-6	£14.99
Lincolnshire (pb)	1-85937-433-6	£9.99	South Wales	1-85937-519-7	£14.99
Liverpool and Merseyside (pb)	1-85937-234-1	£9.99	Southampton (pb)	1-85937-427-1	£9.99
London (pb)	1-85937-183-3	£9.99	Southend (pb)	1-85937-313-5	£9.99
London Living Memories	1-85937-454-9	£14.99	Southport (pb)	1-85937-425-5	£9.99
Ludlow (pb)	1-85937-176-0	£9.99	St Albans (pb)	1-85937-341-0	£9.99
Luton (pb)	1-85937-235-x	£9.99	St Ives (pb)	1-85937-415-8	£9.99
Maidenhead (pb)	1-85937-339-9	£9.99	Stafford Living Memories (pb)	1-85937-503-0	£9.99
Maidstone (pb)	1-85937-391-7	£9.99	Staffordshire (pb)	1-85937-308-9	£9.99
Manchester (pb)	1-85937-198-1	£9.99	Stourbridge (pb)	1-85937-530-8	£9.99
Marlborough (pb)	1-85937-336-4	£9.99	Stratford upon Avon (pb)	1-85937-388-7	£9.99
Middlesex	1-85937-158-2	£14.99	Suffolk (pb)	1-85937-221-x	£9.99
Monmouthshire	1-85937-532-4	£14.99	Suffolk Coast (pb)	1-85937-610-x	£9.99
New Forest (pb)	1-85937-390-9	£9.99	Surrey (pb)	1-85937-240-6	£9.99
Newark (pb)	1-85937-366-6	£9.99	Surrey Living Memories	1-85937-328-3	£14.99
Newport, Wales (pb)	1-85937-258-9	£9.99	Sussex (pb)	1-85937-184-1	£9.99
Newquay (pb)	1-85937-421-2	£9.99	Sutton (pb)	1-85937-337-2	£9.99
Norfolk (pb)	1-85937-195-7	£9.99	Swansea (pb)	1-85937-167-1	£9.99
Norfolk Broads	1-85937-486-7	£14.99	Taunton (pb)	1-85937-314-3	£9.99
Norfolk Living Memories (pb)	1-85937-402-6	£9.99	Tees Valley & Cleveland (pb)	1-85937-623-1	£9.99
North Buckinghamshire	1-85937-626-6	£14.99	Teignmouth (pb)	1-85937-370-4	£7.99
North Devon Living Memories	1-85937-261-9	£14.99	Thanet (pb)	1-85937-116-7	£9.99
North Hertfordshire	1-85937-547-2	£14.99	Tiverton (pb)	1-85937-178-7	£9.99
North London (pb)	1-85937-403-4	£9.99	Torbay (pb)	1-85937-597-9	£9.99
North Somerset	1-85937-302-x	£14.99	Truro (pb)	1-85937-598-7	£9.99
North Wales (pb)	1-85937-298-8	£9.99	Victorian & Edwardian Dorset	1-85937-254-6	£14.99
North Yorkshire (pb)	1-85937-236-8	£9.99	Victorian & Edwardian Kent (pb)	1-85937-624-X	£9.99
Northamptonshire Living Memories	1-85937-529-4	£14.99	Victorian & Edwardian Maritime Album (pb)	1-85937-622-3	£9.99
Northamptonshire	1-85937-150-7	£14.99	Victorian and Edwardian Sussex (pb)	1-85937-625-8	£9.99
Northumberland Tyne & Wear (pb)	1-85937-281-3	£9.99	Villages of Devon (pb)	1-85937-293-7	£9.99
Northumberland	1-85937-522-7	£14.99	Villages of Kent (pb)	1-85937-294-5	£9.99
Norwich (pb)	1-85937-194-9	£8.99	Villages of Sussex (pb)	1-85937-295-3	£9.99
Nottingham (pb)	1-85937-324-0	£9.99	Warrington (pb)	1-85937-507-3	£9.99
Nottinghamshire (pb)	1-85937-187-6	£9.99	Warwick (pb)	1-85937-518-9	£9.99
Oxford (pb)	1-85937-411-5	£9.99	Warwickshire (pb)	1-85937-203-1	£9.99
Oxfordshire (pb)	1-85937-430-1	£9.99	Welsh Castles (pb)	1-85937-322-4	£9.99
Oxfordshire Living Memories	1-85937-525-1	£14.99	West Midlands (pb)	1-85937-289-9	£9.99
Paignton (pb)	1-85937-374-7	£7.99	West Sussex (pb)	1-85937-607-x	£9.99
Peak District (pb)	1-85937-280-5	£9.99	West Yorkshire (pb)	1-85937-201-5	£9.99
Pembrokeshire	1-85937-262-7	£14.99	Weston Super Mare (pb)	1-85937-306-2	£9.99
Penzance (pb)	1-85937-595-2	£9.99	Weymouth (pb)	1-85937-209-0	£9.99
Peterborough (pb)	1-85937-219-8	£9.99	Wiltshire (pb)	1-85937-277-5	£9.99
Picturesque Harbours	1-85937-208-2	£14.99	Wiltshire Churches (pb)	1-85937-171-x	£9.99
Piers	1-85937-237-6	£17.99	Wiltshire Living Memories (pb)	1-85937-396-8	£9.99
Plymouth (pb)	1-85937-389-5	£9.99	Winchester (pb)	1-85937-428-x	£9.99
Poole & Sandbanks (pb)	1-85937-251-1	£9.99	Windsor (pb)	1-85937-333-x	£9.99
Preston (pb)	1-85937-212-0	£9.99	Wokingham & Bracknell (pb)	1-85937-329-1	£9.99
Reading (pb)	1-85937-238-4	£9.99	Woodbridge (pb)	1-85937-498-0	£9.99
Redhill to Reigate (pb)	1-85937-596-0	£9.99	Worcester (pb)	1-85937-165-5	£9.99
Ringwood (pb)	1-85937-384-4	£7.99	Worcestershire Living Memories	1-85937-489-1	£14.99
Romford (pb)	1-85937-319-4	£9.99	Worcestershire	1-85937-152-3	£14.99
Royal Tunbridge Wells (pb)	1-85937-504-9	£9.99	York (pb)	1-85937-199-x	£9.99
Salisbury (pb)	1-85937-239-2	£9.99	Yorkshire (pb)	1-85937-186-8	£9.99
Scarborough (pb)	1-85937-379-8	£9.99	Yorkshire Coastal Memories	1-85937-506-5	£14.99
Sevenoaks and Tonbridge (pb)	1-85937-392-5	£9.99	Yorkshire Dales	1-85937-502-2	£14.99
Sheffield & South Yorks (pb)	1-85937-267-8	£9.99	Yorkshire Living Memories (pb)	1-85937-397-6	£9.99

See Frith books on the internet at www.francisfrith.co.uk

FRITH PRODUCTS & SERVICES

Francis Frith would doubtless be pleased to know that the pioneering publishing venture he started in 1860 still continues today. Over a hundred and forty years later, The Francis Frith Collection continues in the same innovative tradition and is now one of the foremost publishers of vintage photographs in the world. Some of the current activities include:

Interior Decoration

Today Frith's photographs can be seen framed and as giant wall murals in thousands of pubs, restaurants, hotels, banks, retail stores and other public buildings throughout the country. In every case they enhance the unique local atmosphere of the places they depict and provide reminders of gentler days in an increasingly busy and frenetic world.

Product Promotions

Frith products are used by many major companies to promote the sales of their own products or to reinforce their own history and heritage. Frith promotions have been used by Hovis bread, Courage beers, Scots Porage Oats, Colman's mustard, Cadbury's foods, Mellow Birds coffee, Dunhill pipe tobacco, Guinness, and Bulmer's Cider.

Genealogy and Family History

As the interest in family history and roots grows world-wide, more and more people are turning to Frith's photographs of Great Britain for images of the towns, villages and streets where their ancestors lived; and, of course, photographs of the churches and chapels where their ancestors were christened, married and buried are an essential part of every genealogy tree and family album.

Frith Products

All Frith photographs are available Framed or just as Mounted Prints and Posters (size 23 x 16 inches). These may be ordered from the address below. From time to time other products - Address Books, Calendars, Table Mats, etc - are available.

The Internet

Already fifty thousand Frith photographs can be viewed and purchased on the internet through the Frith websites and a myriad of partner sites.

For more detailed information on Frith companies and products, look at these sites:

www.francisfrith.co.uk
www.francisfrith.com
(for North American visitors)

See the complete list of Frith Books at:
www.francisfrith.co.uk
This web site is regularly updated with the latest list of publications from the Frith Book Company. If you wish to buy books relating to another part of the country that your local bookshop does not stock, you may purchase on-line.

For further information, trade, or author enquiries please contact us at the address below:
The Francis Frith Collection, Frith's Barn, Teffont, Salisbury, Wiltshire, England SP3 5QP.
Tel: +44 (0)1722 716 376 Fax: +44 (0)1722 716 881 Email: sales@francisfrith.co.uk

See Frith books on the internet at www.francisfrith.co.uk

FREE MOUNTED PRINT

CHOOSE ANY IMAGE FROM THIS BOOK

Mounted Print
Overall size 14 x 11 inches

Fill in and cut out this voucher and return
it with your remittance for £2.25 (to cover postage and handling). Offer valid for delivery to UK addresses only.

Choose any photograph included in this book.
Your SEPIA print will be A4 in size. It will be mounted in a cream mount with a burgundy rule line (overall size 14 x 11 inches).

Order additional Mounted Prints at HALF PRICE (only £7.49 each*)
If you would like to order more Frith prints from this book, possibly as gifts for friends and family, you can buy them at half price (with no additional postage and handling costs).

Have your Mounted Prints framed
For an extra £14.95 per print* you can have your mounted print(s) framed in an elegant polished wood and gilt moulding, overall size 16 x 13 inches (no additional postage and handling required).

---

* IMPORTANT!

These special prices are only available if you order at the same time as you order your free mounted print. You must use the ORIGINAL VOUCHER on this page (no copies permitted). We can only despatch to one address.

Send completed Voucher form to:
The Francis Frith Collection, Frith's Barn, Teffont, Salisbury, Wiltshire SP3 5QP

 *for FREE and Reduced Price Frith Prints*

Please do not photocopy this voucher. Only the original is valid, so please fill it in, cut it out and return it to us with your order.

Picture ref no	Page no	Qty	Mounted @ £7.49	Framed + £14.95	Total Cost
		1	Free of charge*	£	£
			£7.49	£	£
			£7.49	£	£
			£7.49	£	£
			£7.49	£	£
			£7.49	£	£

Please allow 28 days for delivery

* Post & handling (UK)	£2.25
Total Order Cost	£

Title of this book . . . .

I enclose a cheque/postal order for £ . . . .
made payable to 'The Francis Frith Collection'

OR please debit my Mastercard / Visa / Switch / Amex card
(credit cards please on all overseas orders), details below

Card Number

Issue No (Switch only)   Valid from (Amex/Switch)

Expires   Signature

Name Mr/Mrs/Ms . . . .
Address . . . .
. . . .
. . . .
. . . . Postcode . . . .
Daytime Tel No . . . .
Email . . . .

Valid to 31/12/05

Would you like to find out more about Francis Frith?

We have recently recruited some entertaining speakers who are happy to visit local groups, clubs and societies to give an illustrated talk documenting Frith's travels and photographs. If you are a member of such a group and are interested in hosting a presentation, we would love to hear from you.

Our speakers bring with them a small selection of our local town and county books, together with sample prints. They are happy to take orders. A small proportion of the order value is donated to the group who have hosted the presentation. The talks are therefore an excellent way of fundraising for small groups and societies.

Can you help us with information about any of the Frith photographs in this book?

We are gradually compiling an historical record for each of the photographs in the Frith archive. It is always fascinating to find out the names of the people shown in the pictures, as well as insights into the shops, buildings and other features depicted.

If you recognize anyone in the photographs in this book, or if you have information not already included in the author's caption, do let us know. We would love to hear from you, and will try to publish it in future books or articles.

Our production team

Frith books are produced by a small dedicated team at offices in the converted Grade II listed 18th-century barn at Teffont near Salisbury, illustrated above. Most have worked with the Frith Collection for many years. All have in common one quality: they have a passion for the Frith Collection. The team is constantly expanding, but currently includes:

Jason Buck, John Buck, Douglas Mitchell-Burns, Ruth Butler, Heather Crisp, Isobel Hall, Julian Hight, Peter Horne, James Kinnear, Karen Kinnear, Tina Leary, David Marsh, Sue Molloy, Kate Rotondetto, Dean Scource, Eliza Sackett, Terence Sackett, Sandra Sampson, Adrian Sanders, Sandra Sanger, Julia Skinner, Lewis Taylor, Shelley Tolcher and Lorraine Tuck.